A Little Book
of Poetry:

MASKS

LeMuel Sheppard

PMG Publishing House
c/o TaLisa Sheppard Inc.
138 North Hamilton Road, #177
Gahanna, Ohio 43230

A Little Book of Poetry: Masks
ISBN-13: 978-0692450123   ISBN-10: 0692450122

CONTENTS

1

MASKS

We all have a mask.
You might have more than one.
Like, you have one
when you are trying to have fun.

But what about when you're in public
or when the mask comes off?
Will you be scared of what others think?
Or will you become lost?

Is there a cost
to get another?
Do you put on a mask
when you talk to your mother?

Do you have a mask to mask your feelings?
Like, when you're happy,
do you smile
and show the world how you feel?

Try taking off that mask
Then keep it off
so that people know what's real.

We all have different masks.
Some, you change without knowing.
Or some change automatically.
If you've seen my sad mask,
please don't give it back to me.

Actually when you find it
be careful who it goes to.
It could go to a friend
or someone who doesn't know you.

Don't be afraid to show the old you,
we care, but right now
we wanna see the real you.

So, can your mask come off ?
Should the mask ever come off?
Do people really need to see it?
Well, some of you seem to believe it.

Your mask can't keep your secrets.
What if it's like a monster?
And your secrets just continue to feed it.
So please
put down your mask
and for now
just leave it.

2

BROWN SKIN ME

How is it to be
a brown skin me?

Everywhere I go
people see me differently.

I walk into a fancy store
and I'm soon
stalked by security.

They said they're taking "precautions",
but why didn't they follow the
white kid when he walked in?

I said-
"Sir, please stop followin"
He said-
*"This is a big store
- one you could get lost in"*.

Suddenly
I feel eyes of older women
and gentlemen judging me.

They had an idea of me
as soon as I came in the door-
A brown skin boy
who doesn't belong in this store.

But this little story doesn't bother me,
and I don't lose sleep over it.
I have a point to make
If I didn't
I wouldn't have told you it.

So before y'all judge
all the brown skins
you see-
think about how
it is to be brown skin me.

3

10 MINUTES

Wait a sec-
stop talking.

You don't listen.
You say you a good student
but good students pay attention

What are the cops doing?
Little kids have gone missin.
You better look down and watch your step
So you will stop trippin.
You know everything but
You be looking lost in the kitchen.

Where the bucket at?
This man here is spittin
Officer checked his cup
and found out what he was sippin.

You thots
should be in church
Repentin for all this sinnin
We all can thank God
When this war with Satan
is finished and ended

I ain't a fish
or Michael Phelps
So I won't be going swimming.
But you know...
I've said some things and
done some things that I might resent.
But I'm loyal to one girl
That don't mean I can't pimp.
But my pants don't sag
and I don't walk with a limp
I can only drive with my Mom
cause I only got my temps.

My car is really nice
there's no scratches or dents.
Shout out to all the homeless people
who are living in a tent.
I'm bragging about my car
when y'all would love to pay rent.
I'm sorry for the boasting
and I'm praying for the people
who are begging for cents.

Ya' thoughts are twisted
and kinda' bent
Don't get mad
you know what I meant.

Are you a thug?
Are you thuggin?
Do you want to be a menace?
Imagine how much stuff I could talk about
if I had 10 minutes.

4

ROUTINE

Day 1

Stopped me at a red light
hasn't went green
I been here all night
day hit
I'm starting to think it's a dream.

Or is it a nightmare?
and I'm trapped in this car
but it's nice
so, I don't care.

Somebody pulled up next to me
and just stared.
They got scared
and looked away.
Then the night came
and gone,
now it's another day.

Day 2

I'm still trapped here
like how headlights can trap a deer.
And put them in a trance,
-wait a minute,
I have on a new shirt and pair of pants
or jeans
maybe it wasn't a dream.

Maybe in the scheme of things
we forgot to bring imagination to the table
so it seems
that we need to think
like we are on the brink
of a new discovery.

I'm deep in the ice..
I'm cold.
So cover me.
Being thoughtless is a luxury
no one can afford,
even Bill Gates hates being out of place,
I know he is upset
cause Apple is winning the race.
You say –
"what do you mean?"
I mean take a step back
and to the left
and get out of this
old boring routine.

5
THE MONSTER I'D NEVER SEEN

One night when I was five
I had this crazy dream.
It was about a monster
- one I'd never seen

This monster lived in my closet
I approached it and
thought of something to say
but the monster roared
and I ran away

Terrified of the mysterious beast
I ran back to my bed.
I hid with my stuffed animal friends
and as I pulled the covers over my head.

Maybe it's just hungry, I thought
so I called the pizza place.
Then I hung up,
because I couldn't pay.

I took a deep breath
and told them
"we have to be brave!"
We all took a vote
and chose to sacrifice the turtle
named Dave.

Dave begged me not to-
but something had to be done!
Cause I was not going let
the beast get everyone

I tip toed to the closet
as fast as I can
When I got to it I threw in Dave
and closed the door with my left hand.

.I waited and listened for a noise
but no sound was made.
Either the monster was sleeping,
or he doesn't like Dave.

We waited till it got light outside
then we went to see if our friend
had made it through the night.
We rushed to the door to find
that Dave was quite alright.

My Mom came in
and found me holding Dave
and breathing slow and heavy
she said "Boy, hurry up and get dressed,
your breakfast is ready!".

I got dressed and raced down stairs
to find scrambled eggs,
two toaster strudels
and a dollar on my chair.

I inhaled the food and looked at the dollar
It read "in God we trust".
I fold it up
and put it in my pocket
and hurried to the bus.

While riding on the bus
I thought about how we
survived the night.
I wondered why the monster
didn't put up a fight.

Or maybe-
Just maybe
He would be hungry
tonight.

6

INCREDIBLE

I see people do many things
Crazy things
Things I've never seen.

Things I probably wouldn't do
cause they were too extreme.
Like some people are crazy enough
to steal a wedding ring.

See, it's funny,
cause they're not marrying anyone.
They just carrying a thought of someone
that they thought they loved.
But they tricked you
and you cut them
and that ruined the trust.

Then it got burned to ash
but some people call it dust

Y'all became metal
and it rained
now y'all starting to rust.

I see lust
in her eye
or is that a bug?
You say the door won't budge
but you have to give it a tug.

And if you don't try,
why are you here,
why are you so close?
Get out of my ear.

Well if you don't hear me
then I will stop wasting my time.
If you don't mind
I need you to back up
cause that sandwhich is mine.

You are full of trouble.
It follows you everywhere you go.
You say "I'm sorry"
But that line is getting old.

We could of had something special,
and now we will never know.
Every day there's a miracle-
but we'll never see it though.

We too busy watchin' family guy
and eating cereal.
You know you do,
don't lie!

And if you do lie
you should go to church on Sunday.
That should be an every week thing
like me wearing sweats on hump day.

And who should say it couldn't be,
You havin' a flat screen,
that's considered a luxury.

I'm like a loaded gun
so you really shouldn't mess with me
You can get hurt
and someone should alert
the authorities.

Who are you the dragon or the slayer?
Your boss decided not to pay ya'.
Are you mad or nawh?
You should talk about this problem
But who should you call?
Or you could write about this problem.

But first
are you hungry?
Get a lunchable
Nevermind, it's old and moldy
Now declared inedible.

Let's do an experiment
But it has to be measurable.
We should become
more verbal
and legible.

Now let's do
something amazing
so people will call us
incredible.

7

A BOY NAME PETER

Peter had a mother
but he never got to meet her.
When he did,
he saw the man that was with her.

Peter thought to himself
this man looks like a beater.
He became crazy and became a creeper.
One day the man left and
had a baby by another-
that's makes him a cheater.

Peter knew there was nothing
to do in this situation.
So he sat down and wrote a paper
about the nation
and it's problems.
Then wrote about how we could solve them.

He made a hit list of
the people that caused them.

So the next day he told his Mom
he was going on a run.
Peter went around the block
to the guy who sold guns.

That night, Peter came home
with three different types.
A sniper, an AK-47,
and a pistol with a knife.

You know, for that up close and personal.
Turns out young Peter
was creating a little arsenal.

So after planning and plotting
he set out for his first target.
This was a new Peter.
One that was dark and cold hearted.

He waited till it was dark
and streetlights came on.
Then he crept up slowly
on a man that was on the cell phone.

He said
"Hey! Do you remember me?
cause I remember how you used to cheat
and beat
on my mother.
Why were you even with her?
You never even loved her".

Then Peter asked,
"Do you have anything
that needs to be heard"?

The man didn't know
these would be his last words.

So again, Peter said
"if you have anything to say,
say it! Cause it's gonna be your last."

But before the man could speak,
we all just heard a blast.
The lying cheating man's body
hit the ground fast.
Peter put the gun away
and dragged him to the tall grass.

It was irrational but
he shot the man again,
then looked up as the wind
hit his face.
His cell was ringing and
Peter answered the phone.
They said his Mom
had died that day.

Overwhelmed with tears,
he dropped down next to the dead body,
looked up and yelled
Momma I'm sorry.
I should have been there when you called me.

I see all the pain that you went through,
I never lent a helping hand
but Mom I meant too.
I never told you this
but Momma I love you
and I miss you.

Tell God I said hi
cause I know he is with you.
You know what?
I'm a see you soon.
I'm a try the afterlife
cause this life is ruined

BANG!!

Whoever was around
heard that one last blast.
The question is
why did Peter go bad?
What happen to the old Peter
who use to laugh-
or did he ever really laugh?

What was there to laugh about?
Why didn't anything good
ever come from his mouth?
But finally the truth came out.

Before he ended his life,
he became so heartless.
Tell me why his life ended
before it even started?

8

THE ONE THING

The
one thing I
ever loved, was good
food. The good food that
makes me smile - and makes people ask
what up with you? They didn't know that I just
had a snack or two. The food that I hate - was
the food with no taste. The food that can't be
fixed with salt or pepper. I pray that next time
the food will taste better. The food is important.
So don't burn the good stuff – or   your night
will become rough. Going to   bed hungry,
with no food to eat - will make the night harder
when you can't go to sleep.

9

THE ALIYAH STORY

At the age of seventeen
Aliyah had big aspirations
and big dreams.
One of those dreams
was about meeting her father.
His name is Rick-
a man she thought loved her.
He's actually a man
who never even hugged her.

Her being desperate
for a man's affection,
Aliyah didn't question
any man that said
"I love you".
And she didn't care if it was true.

The men never stayed
And when they leave,
she would cry,

wipe the tears away
then look for someone new.
Then a guy came in
wearin an all white suit.
He said "lil Momma you kinda cute."

He takes her back to his home
on the ride back he said,
"I will never leave you alone"
"You have my word"
They pulled to this gated home
deep in the suburb.
Greeted by two other women
they said they were just
his "friends with benefits."
But these friends never left
A man approached the car with two drinks.
One red, one pink.

Aliyah drunk one without thinking,
then strolled inside.
She found the nearest person
who put their hand between her thighs
She started telling people
to "come get on top of me".
The man in the suit
slipped Aliyah some ecstasy.

After she was done on
her sexual rampage,
she asked for some medicine
cause she had a bad headache.

Then came the man
in the all-white suit

and said
"I have what you need
but you have to sniff it to get better."
Aliyah listened to the man
And sniffs the white powder.
The man in the suit leaves
but comes back in a hour.
To see a young girl
strung out
on the couch
foaming out the mouth.

The man in the suit hesitates
but doesn't shed a tear.
He claps his hands and
two men come.
He orders them to
"get her out of here".

Out of nowhere the cops came in.
The man races to his room
locks the door,
then he says a little prayer.
He gets on the bed and stares
at a picture of his daughter.

"She is gone now
and doesn't know
that I loved her.
I've should have never
left her and her mother."

The cops came into his room
and said "sir come with me!"
but the man didn't listen.

So they put him on his knees.
The cops told the man
that he was sick.
They asked him his name.
He said

"Rick".

10

STRESSED

Stuck in this mindset
Sittin here
Tryin not to become
Mindless

See
We go through a lot
and we are tired
of this stress

But
then we do something crazy
like imagine a zebra in a dress
Ha-ha
That's crazy.

Almost like
the crazy old lady who
tried to feed old milk
to the new born baby.

You know we can
do something special,
but we're just young and lazy
Some people are kinda strict.
I did it wrong
Now you hate me

I've been feeling down lately
I'm ashy
But not pasty
Depressed but not
Insane "B"

Anything is anything
and everything ain't something.

I'm never hungry
but I get force fed
muffins.

You mad
but why you blushin?
It's just a case of incest
Cause you in love
with your cousin.

You can try
to play it off
and act like its nothin.
Or you could blow up
With the push of a button
Whatever you do
Stop with the
Self-destruction.

11

WHITE PRIVILEGE

My skin isn't light
or at least
isn't light enough.
And as you get older
somethings become rough
for us blacks
when we grow up.
Some grow up alone.
Mom made the choice
to keep the little ones
at home
and hiding.
Pops and
the cops fighting.
Brother outside rioting
against the white man.
He pulls out the gun and shoots.
Then gets loud like a hype man.
The police see what happened
But they just look at the man
and take no type of action.

The cop must have seen his skin
They saw that he was white
And they didn't
take him in.
"Come on y'all
You feel me?
Everything isn't cool
in the village!"
I know
everyone has seen
some kind of
white privilege.

12

TIME

Time.
Something we call endless
Tick tock
your running out of
time…
Well,
Do you miss it?
I guess not
Cause you haven't even
looked
at the clock.
Instead of looking up
Look down
at your watch.
Oh,
I forgot.
You think time is unfair.
So you wouldn't have a watch
so why do you care?
Maybe in the beginning
You were lying
Or maybe you were telling the truth
But you just had bad timing

Hmm
Well how did you spend your time
Did you spend your time right?
Going out?
Having the time
of your life?

Time is the thing
you shouldn't
waste.

So have fun.
Go out.
But go at your own pace
Fix your hair and
your shoe lace.

Cause
something that's never late
Is time

I'm keeping track
of mine

You
Should of been
like me and
Not waste your
time.

13

EIGHT DAYS
TILL' TOMORROW

My mother
said to me,
"There's eight days till tomorrow".
She started to weep
and I felt her sorrow.
I could see
the pain in her tears.
the hate
and fear
that lied in her eyes.

She is a strong woman
conquered by emotions.
There is no potion
or drug
that can keep her from
panicking like there is a swarm of bugs
but the boy hugs
his mama
to relieve her from the pain.

She continued to sob.
He continued to hug
and tell his mama that
he loved her
and felt her sorrow.
The boy looked at her
and said
"Mama, after these eight days,
there will be a new
tomorrow".

About the Author
"Me" in 10 Words
By LeMuel Sheppard

I am:

Unique
Outgoing
Funny
Athletic
Witty
Respectful
Gifted
Polite
Curious
Smart

I am:
Me

www.ingramcontent.com/pod-product-compliance
Lightning Source LLC
Chambersburg PA
CBHW020444030426
42337CB00014B/1379